W9-ATF-116

DATE DUE

Yellow Umbrella Books are published by Red Brick Learning
7825 Telegraph Road, Bloomington, Minnesota 55438
http://www.redbricklearning.com

Library of Congress Cataloging-in-Publication Data
Jiménez, Vita.
    [What is in space? Spanish & English]
    What is in space?/by Vita Jiménez = Qué hay en el espacio?/por Vita Jiménez.
    p. cm.
    Summary: "Simple photos and text present what can be found in
outer space"—Provided by publisher.
    Includes index.
    ISBN-13: 978-0-7368-6008-6 (hardcover)
    ISBN-10: 0-7368-6008-8 (hardcover)
    1. Outer space—Exploration—Juvenile literature. I. Title.
II. Title: Qué hay en el espacio?
QB500.262.J5618 2006
919.904—dc22   2005025724

Written by Vita Jiménez
Developed by Raindrop Publishing

Editorial Director: Mary Lindeen
Editor: Jennifer VanVoorst
Photo Researcher: Wanda Winch
Adapted Translations: Gloria Ramos
Spanish Language Consultants: Jesús Cervantes, Anita Constantino
Conversion Assistants: Jenny Marks, Laura Manthe

Photo Credits
Cover: Digital Vision; Title Page: PhotoDisc; Page 4: E.L. Wright
(UCLA)/NASA/DIRBE/COBE; Page 6: NASA/NSSDC; Page 8: PhotoDisc; Page 10:
NASA/NSSDC; Page 12: PhotoDisc; Page 14: Digital Vision; Page 16: PhotoDisc

1 2 3 4 5 6 11 10 09 08 07 06

What Is in Space?

by Vita Jiménez

¿Qué hay en el espacio?

por Vita Jiménez

Yellow Umbrella Books
for early readers

What is in space?

¿Qué hay en el espacio?

The Earth is in space.

La Tierra está en el espacio.

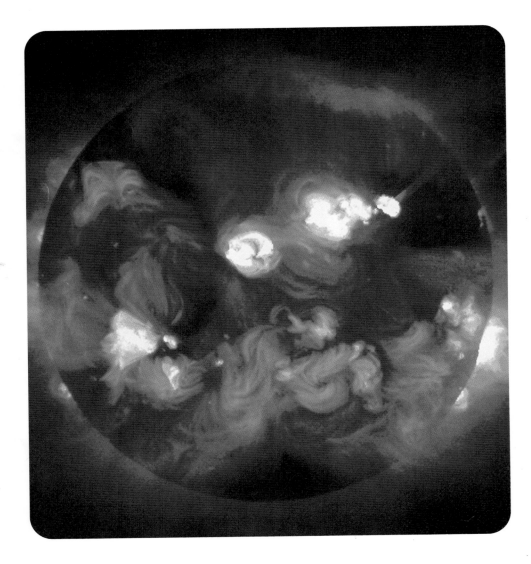

The sun is in space.

El sol está en el espacio.

The moon is in space.

La luna está en el espacio.

The stars are in space.

Las estrellas están en el espacio.

The space shuttle is
in space.

La nave espacial
está en el espacio.

The astronaut is in space.

El astronauta está en el espacio.

Index

Índice